# THE
# DINOSAURS'
# ALPHABET

For Leo
R.F.
For my nephew,
Martin Rogan
J.R.

Look out for the little mammal – our own distant
relative – who lived quietly alongside the dinosaurs.

First edition for the United States, Canada and the Philippines
published 1990 by Barron's Educational Series, Inc.

First published 1990 by Studio Editions Limited, London

Text copyright © Richard Fortey 1990
Illustrations copyright © John Rogan 1990

*All inquiries should be addressed to:*
Barron's Educational Series, Inc.
250 Wireless Boulevard
Hauppauge, New York 11788

International Standard Book No. 0-8120-6202-7

Library of Congress Catalog Card No. 90-43270

Printed and bound in Hong Kong

0123 987654321

# THE
# DINOSAURS'
# ALPHABET

### By Richard Fortey

### Illustrations by John Rogan

**BARRON'S**

New York · Toronto

# A a
## ALLOSAURUS
**Al-oh-saw-rus**

Allo . . . Allo . . .
Allosaurus.
I'm the worst dream
You ever had.
When I feel hungry
I get mad . . .
So, Goodbye, Goodbye,
Allosaurus.

# B b

## BRACHIOSAURUS
**Brack-ee-oh-saw-rus**

I'm huge, I'm vast,
I'm Brachiosaurus – thirty-six feet tall
My brain, I guess, is rather small.
This does not worry me at all –
Would it worry you if you were me,
Eighty tons, tall as a tree?
You couldn't even reach my knee . . .

# Cc

## CHASMOSAURUS
**Kaz-mo-saw-rus**

Isn't my frill thrilling?
Isn't my beak freaky?
My thrilling frill protects my back
From tyrannosaurs' attack;
And then I wander to the creek
And nip off herbs with my freaky beak.

# D d

## DEINONYCHUS
**Dine-on-ik-us**

I'm awful,
I'm clawful,
I'm really not nice.
In fact I'd slice
You through in a trice.
With my claw like a sickle,
I'd cut you up like a pickle!
I'm Deinonychus –
Nobody likes us.

# E e

## EUOPLOCEPHALUS
### Yoo-op-low-kef-al-us

I have armor on my back
I have spikes along my side –
Can you find a little crack
To get inside my hide?
If you think you've found a way
To have a Euoplocephalus steak,
Then I'll hit you with my clubby tail –
You've made a big mistake!

# F f

## FABROSAURUS
**Fab-roe-saw-rus**

I am a friendly kind of beast,
I would not harm you in the least;
It's leaves and shoots I like to munch,
For breakfast, dinner, snack and lunch,
And when I settle for the night,
Eat one last herb with one last bite.

# G g

## GALLIMIMUS
**Gal-ih-mim-us**

If you raced me, you'd be last –
I am really rather fast,
Like a skinny giant bird.
My legs may look absurd,
But they carry me away
To win another day.

# H h

## HYLAEOSAURUS
**Hy-lee-oh-saw-rus**

Who needs brains when you got armor?
When trouble comes along I couldn't be calmer –
When trouble comes along I just sit tight,
Because nothing in the world is going to bite
A creature so spiky and platy,
So impossible-to-breaky.
And when everything is quite all right
I'll go munch a cycadophyte★.

★Cycadophytes (sy-cad-o-fites) are
plants popular with herbivorous dinosaurs.

# I i ICHTHYOSAURUS

**Ick-thee-oh-saw-rus**

I'm not Itchy-osaurus
I'm not Twitchy-osaurus
I'm Ichthyosaurus,
The great sea lizard:
Eyes like saucers,
Pointy teeth.
I take fish in my gizzard
And dive beneath
The wide Jurassic silver sea:
No dolphin dove as well as me!

# J j

## JUBBULPURIA
**Jub-ul-poo-ria**

I'm Jubbulpuria from Jubbulpur
A very Indian dinosaur.
I'm not well known and I'm rather obscure,
Unless they dig me up some more
In Jubbulpur.

# K k

## KENTROSAURUS
**Ken-tro-saw-rus**

My plates and spikes
Are what I likes,
Because they save me from the jaws
Of the nasty carnosaurs:
So don't you come too close, my friend
Or I'll bump you with my spiky end!

# LAMBEOSAURUS

**Lam-bee-oh-saw-rus**

Dinosaurs with crests
Are best!
I blow mine like a horn
To warn
My browsing mate
Of all the dinosaurs we hate –
Those carnosaurs
With toothy jaws
And no respect for decent laws.

# M m

## MAIASAURA
**My-a-saw-ra**

Just like a hen I tend my nest
To hatch my reptile chicks.
And like a hen I'll fuss and cluck
And prod and push with my bill like a duck
When my chicks are in a fix.

# N n

## NODOSAURUS
**Node-oh-saw-rus**

I'm a dumpy tank,
A grumpy tank
And so I'll thank
You leave me be.
So please don't joke
And don't provoke
I just wish folk
Would leave me be.
I'm Nodosaurus –
The No Go Saurus!

# OURANOSAURUS
**Oo-ran-oh-saw-rus**

You cannot fail
To admire my sail.
It serves me very well
In the desert where I dwell,
To take away the heat
From my overheated feet.
Yes – my sail is really neat,
My sail is really swell.

# P p

## PACHYCEPHALOSAURUS
**Pak-ee-kef-al-oh-saw-rus**

My name is long – my skull is thick –
Go on! Try it! Hit me with a brick!
I use my skull for butting
When I'm fighting and strutting,
But after I am done
I don't remember nuttin' –
Not even my own long name!

# Q q

## QUETZALCOATLUS
**Kwet-zal-kote-lus**

Quetzalcoatlus, Quetzalcoatlus!

I fly like a plane but I'm utterly motorless.

They think I am too huge to fly

But I do – and leave them wondering why . . .

So, if you like pondering impossible things,

Consider the size* of my leathery wings.

*Quetzalcoatlus has the wingspan of
a small plane.

# R
# r

## RUTIODON
**Roo-ti-o-don**

I am a Triassic 'gator*
I lurk in the water.
If I don't get you now
Then I'll get you later.

*Rutiodon looks like an alligator,
but is really a different kind of reptile.

# S s

## STYRACOSAURUS
**Sty-rack-oh-saw-rus**

Styracosaurus is my name –
My nature's very sweet.
Plants and herbs I chomp like crazy
I really don't eat meat!
Some people say I look like a rhinoceros
But personally I think
That's quite preposterous!

# T t

## TYRANNOSAURUS
**Tie-ran-oh-saw-rus**

Tyrannosaurus rex am I!
And rex means king
And that is why
I wear a wide and vicious grin.
Yes! Rex means king
Of all the Cretaceous,
So watch out! My appetite's
Always voracious.

# U u

## "ULTRASAURUS"
### Ull-tra-saw-rus

I'm the greatest of all
Bigger than Brachio – vaster than Diplodocus★ –
I'm sixty-five feet tall,
I don't tolerate no hocus-pocus!

★Ultrasaurus is comparing himself with
Diplodocus, one of the longest of all dinosaurs, but
with relatively the smallest brain!

# V v

## VELOCIRAPTOR

**Vel-o-ci-rap-tor**

I'm speedy,
I'm greedy,
I'll soon be your captor –
I'm Velociraptor.
So watch out all you little fauna
Or I'll chase you into
A nasty corner.

# W
# W

## WUERHOSAURUS
**Woo-er-o-saw-rus**

Small of brain and very slow,
I've not got much "get up and go"
And rather more "stand up and stay"
Or "wait for you to go away,"
But as I eat Cretaceous weeds –
A tiny brain is all I needs.

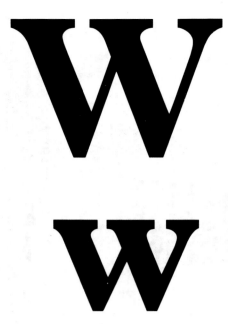

# X
# X

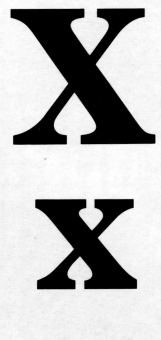

## XIAOSAURUS
**Sheeyow-saw-rus**

A rare dinosaur I –
For I start with an 'x',
Which makes me x-ceptional, x-citing
And x-tra special . . .

So watch me running and leaping and biting
In China long before Pandas and men:
Because I'm x-tinct
And I'll not come again.

# Y y

## YANGCHUANOSAURUS
**Yang-chew-an-oh-saw-rus**

I polish my teeth in the morning
I polish my claws at noon.
Then I gobble my prey
For the rest of the day
And sleep it off under the moon.

# Zz

## ZEPHYROSAURUS
**Zef-eye-roe-saw-rus**

I may be the last
But I'm slim and I'm fast.
Running like the wind,
I leave tyrannosaurs behind:
I'm the dinosaur gazelle!
And so . . . farewell,
Farewell.

# DINOSAUR WORDS

## Armored dinosaurs

These dinosaurs are protected by thick bony plates and spikes.

## Carnosaurs

Dinosaurs who like to eat meat.

## Cycad

Primitive plant often with palm-like leaves, common at the time during which the dinosaurs lived.

## Crest

Growth on the heads of some dinosaurs.

## Duck-billed dinosaurs

These dinosaurs have specially shaped jaws very like a duck's bill.

## Extinct

Dead and gone forever.

## Fauna

All the different kinds of animals.

## Frill

Bony neck-shield.

# Herbivores

Plant-eating animals.

# Ichthyosaurs

Not really dinosaurs, but sea-living reptiles.

# Mammal

Furry animals that produce milk to feed their young. Although they lived alongside the dinosaurs, they did not get a chance to grow large until after the dinosaurs had died out.

# Paleontologist

Scientist who studies fossils, including dinosaurs.

# Pterosaurs

Not really dinosaurs, but flying reptiles. Quetzalcoatlus is a pterosaur.

# WHEN THE DINOSAURS LIVED

The dinosaurs lived during three periods of geological time:

The Cretaceous (Cret-ay-shus) 140-65 million years ago

The Jurassic (Joo-rass-ic) 205-140 million years ago

The Triassic (Try-ass-ic) 245-205 million years ago

The dinosaurs became extinct at the end of the Cretaceous period, 65 million years ago.

The dinosaurs that appear in this book were not all alive at the same time.